The Milky Way and Other Galaxies

By Gregory Vogt

OUR UNIVERSE

www.raintreepublishers.co.uk

Visit our website to find out more information about Raintree books.

To order:

☎ Phone 44 (0)1865 888112

🖹 Send a fax to 44 (0)1865 314091

🖵 Visit the Raintree Bookshop at www.raintreepublishers.co.uk to browse our catalogue and order online.

Design: Jo Hinton-Malivoire and Tinstar Design (www.tinstar.co.uk), Jo Sapwell (www.tipani.co.uk)
Illustrations: Art Construction
Picture Research: Maria Joannou and Su Alexander
Production: Jonathan Smith

Originated by Dot Gradations Ltd
Printed and bound in Hong Kong, China by South China Printing Co. Ltd.

ISBN 1 844 21414 1 (hardback)
06 05 04 03 02
10 9 8 7 6 5 4 3 2 1

British Cataloguing in Publication Data

Vogt, Gregory
The Milky Way and other galaxies.– (Our universe)
1. Galaxies – Juvenile literature 2. Milky Way – Juvenile literature
I. Title
523.1'13
A full catalogue record for this book is available from the British Library.

Acknowledgements
The publishers would like to thank the following for permission to reproduce photographs:
Cover Photo; G. Fritz Benedict (University of Texas) and NASA, title page; T.A.Rector, B.Wolpa, M.Hanna, KPNO 0.9-m Mosaic, AURA/ NOAO/NSF, 9; Hubble Heritage Team (AURA/STScI/ NASA), 6, 16, 22, 24, 35, 36, 40; European Southern Observatory, 10, 20, 28, 32, 39; Roger Ressmeyer/ CORBIS, 18; Roeland P. van der Marel (STScI), Frank C. van den Bosch (University of Washington), and NASA, 12; NASA, 14, 16, 19, 26, 33; B.Whitmore (STScI) and NASA, 30; K. Borne (STScI) and NASA, 33; Bill Schoening, Vanessa Harvey/REU program/AURA/NOAO/NSF, 42; NASA/JPL, 44.

Content Consultant
David Jewitt
Professor of Astronomy
University of Hawaii Institute for Astronomy

Every effort has been made to contact copyright holders of any material reproduced in this book. Any omissions will be rectified in subsequent printings if notice is given to the publishers.

Contents

Any words appearing in the text in bold, **like this**, are explained in the glossary.

Diagram of the Milky Way

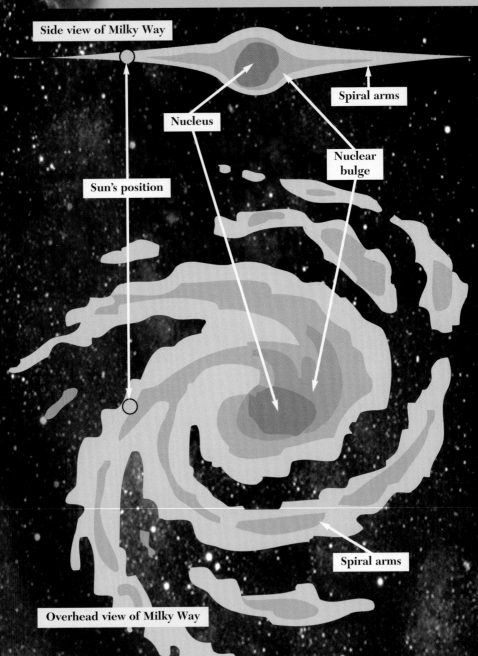

Side view of Milky Way

Spiral arms

Nucleus

Nuclear bulge

Sun's position

Spiral arms

Overhead view of Milky Way

A quick look at galaxies

What is a galaxy?
A galaxy is a very large system of gas and dust clouds called **nebulas**, stars and objects that orbit stars.

What holds a galaxy together?
All the objects in a galaxy are held together by **gravity**. Gravity is a force that attracts objects to each other.

What do galaxies look like?
Galaxies can be many shapes and sizes. Some look like circles. Others look like large **spirals**. Other galaxies have no certain shapes. These galaxies may look like lumpy clouds.

What is the Milky Way?
The Earth is in a galaxy known as the Milky Way. Scientists think it is shaped like a giant spiral.

This group of stars is near the centre of the Milky Way Galaxy.

About galaxies

A galaxy is a very large group of millions of solar systems. A solar system is a star and all the objects that orbit around it. Stars are giant balls of hot gases that give off light and heat. Objects in galaxies are always moving through outer space.

Astronomers are scientists who study objects in space. They believe there are billions of galaxies. Some astronomers say galaxies are like cities of stars. Vast stretches of empty space separate galaxies from each other.

Each galaxy is different. Galaxies have different sizes and shapes, and they contain different numbers of stars. The Earth is part of the Milky Way Galaxy. The Milky Way has billions of stars.

Objects in galaxies

Gravity forms galaxies and holds them together. Gravity is a force that attracts objects to each other. The gravity of stars and other objects pulls them towards each other to form a galaxy. Gravity makes objects orbit (circle around) other objects instead of drifting away into other parts of space. It also makes objects rotate, or spin.

Galaxies are made up of many different objects. Stars are the most common objects in galaxies. Each star is different. A star's colour depends on how hot it is. Some stars are small and others are giants. Each star goes through a life cycle. The stages of a star are birth, life and death. Stars are born and die in **nebulas**.

Nebulas are thick clouds of gas and dust. Sometimes explosions push gas and dust into clouds. At other times, gravity pulls gas and dust together. In some places, the gas and dust form clumps. Clumps can continue to grow for millions of years. Many of these gas and dust clumps become stars.

▶ **This is a nebula called the Rosette Nebula. New stars forming inside the nebula heat up its gases and make them glow.**

Planets are also a part of galaxies. The Earth is a planet that orbits a star called the Sun. There are other stars that also have planets orbiting them.

Smaller objects also travel within galaxies. Moons are large balls of rock or ice that circle planets. **Asteroids** are huge rocks that travel through space. Comets are clusters of ice and rock that have tails of gases that glow when they are warmed by a star's heat. Asteroids and comets orbit stars.

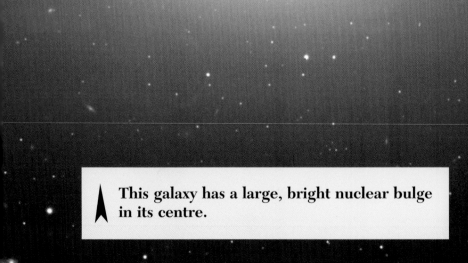

This galaxy has a large, bright nuclear bulge in its centre.

Parts of a galaxy

Most galaxies have the same kind of structure. The shape and size of the structure depends on the kind of galaxy.

The **nucleus** is the centre of a galaxy. Every object in the galaxy orbits around the nucleus. It takes an object millions of years to orbit the nucleus once.

Some scientists believe that **black holes** are at the centre of some galaxies. A black hole is a region of space with an extremely strong **gravitational** pull. It has such great gravity that nothing can escape from it, not even light. The gravity of black holes pulls in anything that comes close to them.

A nuclear bulge is near the centre of the nucleus. Millions of old stars are packed tightly together in the nuclear bulge. They are so close that they often crash into each other.

A disc made of gas and dust surrounds a galaxy's nucleus. Sometimes the gas and dust pack together to form **nebulas**, where new stars form.

A halo of stars surrounds the disc. The stars in the halo are far away from each other. Most halo stars are old stars from when the galaxy first formed.

The corona is the outer part of a galaxy. Scientists do not know what makes up a galaxy's corona.

Light years

Astronomers use a special measurement for huge distances between objects in space. The measurement is called a light year. This is the distance light travels in one year. A light year equals about 9.5 trillion km (6 trillion miles). The nearest star to the Sun is Proxima Centauri. It is about 40 trillion km (25 trillion miles) away. Measured in light years, Proxima Centauri is 4.2 light years away.

 Scientists believe black holes like this one provide energy for quasars.

Quasars

Quasars are a part of some galaxies. Astronomers are not exactly sure what quasars are. Some scientists believe that a quasar is the **nucleus** of a new galaxy. They believe this because quasars are small but extremely bright.

Quasars give off huge amounts of energy. They release more energy than hundreds of normal galaxies combined. They are so bright that they block the light of other nearby stars.

Astronomers believe quasars have energy because they are near **black holes**. Stars and dust heat up as they are pulled into black holes. They release waves of energy. Scientists believe some of this energy turns on quasars and keeps them shining.

Quasars are billions of light years away from the Earth. They are some of the oldest and the most distant objects that astronomers have discovered in the universe. They are so far away that their light takes billions of years to reach the Earth. That means that when astronomers look at quasars, they are seeing quasar light that is billions of years old.

Light from thousands of stars shines on the Earth. This white stream of stars is the Milky Way.

and the other planets and moons in our solar system are part of the Milky Way Galaxy. Billions of stars outside our solar system are also part of the Milky Way.

On some nights, you can see a faint white band in the sky. People named the band the Milky Way because it is white like milk. Millions of stars from inside the Milky Way give the band its milky white glow.

The Milky Way contains at least 100 billion stars. From edge to edge, it is about 80,000 to 100,000 light years across.

Scientists believe that the Milky Way has spiral arms like this galaxy.

Parts of the Milky Way

The younger stars of the Milky Way are arranged in a big disc. The disc is about 2000 light years thick. The older stars are in the nuclear bulge of the Milky Way. This is a bright cluster of stars that looks like a large ball from far away.

The **nucleus** is in the centre of the bulge. Some scientists believe that there may be a **black hole** in the nucleus of the Milky Way.

Studying the Milky Way's arms

Astronomers cannot see the entire Milky Way. The whole galaxy is hard to see because the Earth is inside it. Astronomers use telescopes to study the small parts of the galaxy that they can see. A telescope makes distant objects look clearer and closer.

Astronomers have learned more about the Milky Way by comparing it to other galaxies. They have found that small clusters of stars are coming out of the nucleus of the Milky Way. The clusters stretch out from the nucleus and form long arm-like structures. The arms **spiral** around the nucleus.

Astronomers named each of the Milky Way's arms. The arms include the Orion Arm, the Perseus Arm and the Sagittarius Arm. These arms are named after heroes from Greek and Roman legends.

The Sun is located in one of the spiral arms of the galaxy. It is about 26,000 light years away from the centre of the galaxy.

Stars like the Sun and many other objects orbit the centre of the Milky Way. It takes the Sun about 250 million years to orbit the centre once. Scientists call this amount of time a galactic year.

This is one of the most famous star groups in the Milky Way. It is called the Pleiades Star Cluster, or the Seven Sisters. People can see it from the Earth without using telescopes.

Myths about the Milky Way

In ancient times, people saw the stars in the sky, but they could not study them the way scientists do today. The tools astronomers use today had not been invented. Instead, people told stories called myths to explain the movements of stars, planets and galaxies.

Ancient peoples saw the milky white band of stars in the sky. They did not know that the band was really the Milky Way Galaxy. People told stories to explain how the white band of light came to be in the sky.

Greek people told a myth about Hera. She was the queen of the gods. Her milk sprayed into the sky and formed the Milky Way. The word 'galaxy' also comes from this myth. *Gala* means milk in the Greek language.

In Africa, some people believed that the Milky Way was like a wall. They believed that animals of darkness lived on the other side of the wall. The wall stopped the monsters from coming to Earth.

This is a large, barred-spiral galaxy.

Kinds of galaxies

There are three main kinds of galaxies. Each kind of galaxy has a different shape.

A **spiral galaxy** is named after its arms. It has large arms made up of stars. The arms spiral around the centre of the galaxy. The arms may be tightly or loosely wound around the galaxy's centre.

There are two kinds of spiral galaxies. Open spirals have a large flat disc. Long spiral arms circle outward from the nuclear bulge. The arms look like a Catherine wheel. They are made up of many bright, young stars. Astronomers believe that the Milky Way is an open spiral galaxy.

A barred-spiral galaxy has a thick strip of stars running through its nuclear bulge. The spiral arms start at the ends of the strip instead of from the bulge.

> This picture of deep space shows different kinds of galaxies. The round-shaped ones are elliptical galaxies.

Elliptical galaxies

Elliptical galaxies are the most common kind of galaxy. They have no arms. They are made up of one large ball of stars. Some elliptical galaxies are round like a football. Others are oval like a rugby ball.

Elliptical galaxies are made mainly of old stars. There is only a little gas and dust in elliptical galaxies. There is not enough gas and dust to form **nebulas** that make new stars.

Stars move differently in elliptical galaxies than they do in spiral galaxies. Spiral galaxies and barred-spiral galaxies get their shape because of how they are turning. Each star orbits around the **nucleus**. Stars that are near the nucleus orbit faster than stars that are further away. The stars' orbits group them into spiral-shaped arms. But the stars in elliptical galaxies do not orbit in a regular pattern around the centre. Instead, they orbit in different directions and at different speeds.

Most elliptical galaxies are small and dim. These small galaxies are called dwarfs. Dwarfs can contain about 100 million stars. They are only a few hundred light years across. Many of the nearest galaxies to the Milky Way are dwarfs.

However, a few elliptical galaxies are giants or supergiants. They can be as large as 5 million light years across. These giant galaxies contain billions of stars. The light from the stars makes the galaxies very bright.

This irregular galaxy is the Large Magellanic Cloud.

Irregular galaxies

Some galaxies have no clear shape and no central bulge of stars. These are called **irregular galaxies**. They look like bumpy masses of stars. Irregular galaxies are smaller than most other kinds of galaxies. They usually have fewer stars. They are hard for astronomers to see because they are small and dim. This makes it hard for astronomers to find them.

Irregular galaxies contain lots of gas and dust. They look like they are surrounded by fog.

In 1521, the Portuguese explorer Ferdinand Magellan was sailing far to the south on a trip around the world. At night, he spotted two clouds that looked like faint patches of light. Sailors on this trip were the first to describe the clouds to scientists in Europe. Around 1930, astronomers discovered that the clouds were really irregular galaxies. These galaxies were named the Magellanic Clouds after the explorer.

The Magellanic Clouds are close to the Milky Way. These galaxies are about 180,000 light years away from the Earth. Their closeness makes them easy to see from the southern half of the Earth.

The Large Magellanic Cloud contains about 15 billion stars. The Small Magellanic Cloud has fewer stars. A huge band of **hydrogen** gas surrounds the clouds. The band of gas is called the Magellanic Stream.

Galaxy clusters

Most galaxies are found in groups called clusters. Small clusters can have anything from a few to hundreds of galaxies in them. Larger clusters contain thousands of galaxies.

The Milky Way Galaxy is part of a small cluster of galaxies called the Local Group. There are about 40 galaxies in this group. The Andromeda Galaxy and the Magellanic Clouds are also part of the cluster.

The Virgo Cluster is about 50 million light years away from the Earth, beyond the Milky Way. This cluster can be found in the sky near the Virgo **constellation**. A constellation is a group of stars that forms a pattern in a certain part of the sky. The Virgo Cluster has about 3000 galaxies.

The largest galaxy clusters are called superclusters. They are made up of tens of thousands of galaxies.

This small cluster of galaxies is called the Hickson Compact Group. The cluster contains several spiral galaxies and an elliptical galaxy.

Astronomers believe this galaxy got its odd shape when an elliptical galaxy joined a spiral galaxy.

Changing galaxies

Galaxies can stay the same or change very slowly. Astronomers cannot tell if, when or how a galaxy will change. An **elliptical galaxy** could end up looking like a **spiral galaxy**. It might become an **irregular galaxy**. Or it might not change much at all.

Sometimes **gravity** changes the shape of galaxies. When two galaxies pass each other, each pulls on the other. This gravitational pull can change the shape of both galaxies.

Gas and dust in the galaxies are pulled around by gravity. Moving the gas and dust can make many **nebulas** form. Many stars start forming in these nebulas at once. Galaxies with many new stars forming are called starburst galaxies.

This photograph shows two galaxies that are colliding with each other.

Colliding galaxies

Sometimes galaxies collide, or run into each other. Stars in colliding galaxies rarely touch each other. Galaxies are mostly empty space. The stars in galaxies are very far away from each other. The stars of one colliding galaxy simply pass by the stars of the other.

Each galaxy changes, even though the stars do not crash into each other. A galaxy with more mass has greater **gravity** than a galaxy with less mass. Mass is the amount of matter an object contains. A galaxy with a great deal of mass, or material, is called massive.

The gravity of the massive galaxy may pull in some of the stars from the less massive galaxy. The gravity may also pull gas and dust from one galaxy into the other.

When galaxies collide, their shapes may also change. Gravity could cause the orbits of the stars in an **irregular galaxy** to begin to **spiral**. In time, the irregular galaxy could become a spiral galaxy.

This photograph shows what a ring galaxy looks like.

Ring galaxies

Sometimes when galaxies collide, their shapes will change into a ring. There are very few ring-shaped galaxies because it takes special conditions to make them. To make a ring galaxy, a smaller galaxy must hit the bigger galaxy directly in the centre. This does not happen often, so ring galaxies are rare.

The Cartwheel Galaxy is a ring galaxy. It has a bright **nucleus** of stars. Several small arms come out

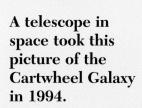

A telescope in space took this picture of the Cartwheel Galaxy in 1994.

from the centre like spokes on a wheel, and a ring surrounds the spokes. The ring is about 100,000 light years in diameter. Diameter is the distance from one side of a sphere or circle to the other, passing through the centre. The Cartwheel Galaxy contains several billion stars.

The Cartwheel Galaxy got its ring-galaxy shape when it collided with another galaxy. A smaller galaxy travelled through it. Gas in the larger galaxy was squeezed into a large ring by the **gravity** of the small galaxy. This caused many new stars to form in the ring. The new stars glow brightly. This makes it easy for astronomers to see the ring from the Earth.

Galactic cannibalizing

Cannibalizing is taking parts from something to make or fix something else. Galactic cannibalizing happens when the **gravity** of one large galaxy sucks a smaller galaxy into it. Some or all of the smaller galaxy becomes part of the large galaxy.

Galactic cannibalizing occurs very slowly. Some galaxies are only partly 'eaten' by larger galaxies. Other galaxies are completely swallowed by larger galaxies.

When a large galaxy collides with a smaller galaxy, their stars slide right past each other, but the small galaxy does not get away. The gravity of the large galaxy slows it down. The gravity pulls the small galaxy back into the large galaxy.

The large galaxy rips away the small galaxy's gas and dust. Its outer stars begin to orbit in the large galaxy. Finally, the small galaxy stops moving away from the large galaxy. The two galaxies join to make one galaxy.

This photograph shows how a large galaxy is
eating a small galaxy.

This picture shows a sideways view of one spiral galaxy behind another galaxy. Scientists need telescopes to study these galaxies.

Studying galaxies

In ancient times, it was hard for people to study stars closely without telescopes. Many stars were too far away for them to see just with their eyes.

Scientists Hans Lippershey and Galileo Galilei made the first telescopes in 1608 and 1609. Galileo made many discoveries about stars with his telescope. He studied the Milky Way and learned that the milky band was really the combined light of countless stars.

Over the next centuries, scientists improved telescopes. This helped astronomers make new discoveries about the Milky Way. Astronomer Thomas Wright discovered that the Milky Way was shaped like a disc. Other astronomers began trying to measure the size of the Milky Way. Some thought it was 30,000 light years across. Others thought it was 200,000 light years across.

How telescopes work

Optical telescopes work by collecting light energy. Telescopes that collect greater amounts of light are more powerful than those that collect little light.

There are two ways optical telescopes collect light. Reflecting telescopes use curved mirrors to catch light. A mirror at the back end of the telescope bounces light to another small mirror. This small mirror then reflects the light to an eyepiece or to a camera. Cameras form pictures from the light.

Refracting telescopes use lenses to aim the light. A big lens is at the telescope's front end. It focuses light like a magnifying glass to make an image. The smaller lens, or eyepiece, makes the image larger.

Stars give off other kinds of light energy besides the kind people can see, including radio waves, X-rays and ultraviolet rays. This energy travels through space as waves. Scientists use special telescopes to study these waves of energy.

A radio telescope uses a large dish to collect radio waves. The dish focuses the waves and bounces them on to a detector. The detector changes the radio waves to signals that a computer can read. Then it sends the radio signals to the computer. The computer uses the signals to create pictures that scientists can study.

Today, telescopes are much larger than they were in the past. These workers are taking the covering off a huge mirror. The mirror will be put in a large telescope. The telescope is kept in a building called an observatory. There are many observatories around the world.

Astronomer Edwin Hubble used Cepheid variables like the ones in this spiral galaxy to measure the distances between galaxies.

Edwin Hubble

Edwin Hubble (1889–1953) was an astronomer who made many discoveries about galaxies. Until the 1920s, astronomers believed that the Milky Way was the only galaxy. Hubble proved that there was more than one galaxy. He also discovered that galaxies travel through space.

Hubble spotted Cepheid variables in distant galaxies. He watched to see how long they took to change. This helped him measure their brightest point. He used this brightest point to learn how far away they were.

Galaxies move away from each other because the universe is expanding, or spreading out. Hubble used mathematics to figure out how fast galaxies are moving away from each other. His mathematical formula is called the Hubble Constant.

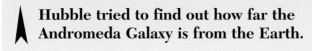

Hubble tried to find out how far the Andromeda Galaxy is from the Earth.

Andromeda Galaxy

For many years, people thought the Andromeda Galaxy was a **nebula**. But Edwin Hubble learned that it was a galaxy like the Milky Way.

The Andromeda Galaxy is a **spiral galaxy** found in the sky near the **constellation** Andromeda. It has two **nuclei** and it is the largest galaxy in the Local Group. It is also the most distant object people can see from the Earth without using a telescope.

Hubble used his method for measuring distances to find out how far away the Andromeda Galaxy is. He discovered Cepheid variable stars in the Andromeda Galaxy. He found out their brightness and from that, he determined that the galaxy was about one million light years away. However, the Cepheid-variable method for measuring distance was not perfect.

Today, astronomers measure red shift of stars and galaxies to learn distance. Red shift is the way light changes as objects move away from each other in space. Stars moving away from the Earth appear slightly red. The light appears redder when the stars move away from each other quickly.

Astronomers compare red shifts of different stars and galaxies. They use this information to find out the distances of objects that are travelling away from each other in space. Astronomers used red shift to discover that the Andromeda Galaxy is actually about 2.25 million light years away from the Earth.

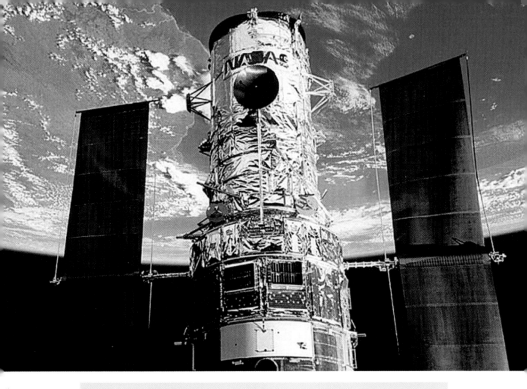

The Hubble Space Telescope was named after Edwin Hubble.

Telescopes

The telescope Edwin Hubble used to study galaxies is in California, in the USA, on the top of Mount Wilson. The telescope uses a large mirror 2.4 metres (8 feet) across to collect light. The mirror can collect about 40,000 times more light than a human eye. The mirror reflects light to a camera, and the camera forms pictures from the light.

Today, many telescopes are more than twice as big as Hubble's telescope. Each telescope is located on a

Big Bang

Scientists hope that they will learn more about how the universe started by studying galaxies. Most scientists believe that all the material in the universe was once tightly packed into a very tiny space. They think all the material began to expand rapidly at a moment called the Big Bang. They believe the universe is still expanding today. Scientists are trying to find out how fast the universe is expanding by using the Hubble Constant and the red shift of galaxies. They hope new information might help them learn what the universe will be like in the future.

mountain. The Earth's atmosphere blurs images of stars. An atmosphere is a layer of gases that surrounds an object in space. There is less atmosphere above high places, so telescopes can create clearer images.

The best telescope for studying galaxies is the Hubble Space Telescope, named after Edwin Hubble. This telescope is a spacecraft that orbits the Earth. It can see further and take clearer pictures because it is above the Earth's atmosphere. The telescope sends its pictures back to the Earth by radio. Scientists are studying pictures from the Hubble Space Telescope to discover even more new galaxies.

Glossary

asteroid (AS-tuh-roid) giant space rock

black hole object in space with so much gravity that nothing can escape from it, not even light

constellation group of stars that forms a pattern in the sky

elliptical galaxy group of stars that can be round or flat-shaped

gravity force that attracts all objects to each other

hydrogen lightest element in the universe; hydrogen is an odourless gas

irregular galaxy galaxy with no nucleus, central bulge or clear shape

nebula (NEB-yoo-lah) cloud of gas and dust where stars form

nucleus (NU-klee-uhs) centre of a galaxy

spiral galaxy disc-shaped galaxy with arms that wind around the nucleus

Further information

Websites

BBC Science
http://www.bbc.co.uk/science/space/
British National Space Centre
http://www.bnsc.gov.uk/
European Space Agency
http://sci.esa.int/
**Star Child: A Learning Centre for
          Young Astronomers**
http://starchild.gsfc.nasa.gov/

Books

*Exploring the solar system: Asteroids, Meteors and
    Comets*, Giles Sparrow (Heinemann Library, 2001)
The Universe: Stars and Constellations, Raman Prinja
    (Heinemann Library, 2002)

Useful address

London Planetarium
Marylebone Road
London
NW1 5LR

Index